To Patty,
With all very best wishes
& hoping you enjoy a
jaunt along
Memory Lane!
Pamela
Blanchfield

illustration from 'Hill and the Long Road' page 42

Along

A Long

Memory Lane

40 Poems by

Pamela Blanchfield

illustrated

Contact: sales@keyprints.plus.com

ISBN: 978-1-3999-8208-5

With grateful thanks to my wonderful brother John Blanchfield for his ever-patient and brilliantly analytical help with print preparation

For John, with love

Cover design Pamela Blanchfield

Sometimes I've heard it said, people return to their childhood memories more as time passes, and age delivers details long-forgotten. In my case the details related here have stayed vividly in mind throughout. The poems are about my life and events up to the age of ten, and I believe if we all look back, we can find the roots and formation of our character traits present within our experiences, instinct and actions there.

Contents

Almost Young Forever 11
Life Drawing 13
Noël and Harold 14
Lucky 16
The Old Village 18
Heathen 20
A Long Summer 21
Large and Small 22
Hypocrisy 24
Bow and Arrow 26
A Special Trait 30
Ingredients 32
Nature's Child 35
George 36
The Loveliest Thing 38
Remembering... 41
Hill and the Long Road 42
How I Longed 46
Inequality 48
Sweet Treats 50
High and Low 53
Claustrophobia 54
Cat Lady 56
Aversion 60
My Great Grandparents 62
Victorian 65

The Old Market..66
Points of Pain..69
Young Spirit..72
Wychwood..76
High Heels..78
Creep..80
The Joker..82
Two Friends..83
Show Me...86
Teachers..88
Headline News..92
Different Ways..94
Connections..98
The Arno..100
Other books by Pamela Blanchfield..104
About the author and illustrator..105

Almost Young Forever

I almost stayed young forever, destined not to grow old
And though not remembered by me, this is what I was told:
My family had packed, set to leave the bustling city
And that day was to verge very near to catastrophe,
We were going over the river, to our new home there,
The van made ready, Nanna with me on a rocking chair,
Just a babe in arms, chair in the back, the journey began,
All other possessions were strapped down, secured in the van,
And we travelled along safely, sitting quietly some while
As the removal van sped covering big city miles,
The tail board was fastened, but then something went very wrong:
Six months old in Nanna's arms, and we two rocking along,
The furniture had all been tied up and boxes secured
But not the chair, then the catch broke and opened the tail board,
And we were seen edging nearer towards wide open road
As the driver oblivious sped on fast with his load,
Alarmed motorists gestured, panicked, tried to swiftly warn,
Waving and weaving and frantically honking their horns,
All the time us to the opening gradually creeping
With a cacophony of car horns furiously beeping,
As we hovered helpless in that chair at the precipice
The driver heard, stopped, and prevented a very near miss.
I'm so thankful his foot hit that brake before things went wrong
Or I might never have even reached the grand age of one,

That day our dilemma was averted just on the brink,

We were rescued by the angels who came to us, I think...

Life Drawing

When I was very small
I drew nudes true, from life:
Only of mum and dad,
So, obviously enthralled,
Observed, husband and wife,
Pure nature early, called…
Strange no drawings survived!

Noël and Harold

Noël: certain name of Christmas, long ago,
And Harold too, the pair appeared without fail,
Both laden with such kind gifts for us as children,
Noël boasted: "all bought in the January sale!"

Some things they hand-crafted, were skilfully made:
I recall a small wooden shop, with jars of sweets,
Two family friends known to us as uncles
Whose beaming smiles appeared with seasonal treats

Bachelor pals – evening dusk, the pair arrived:
Once I was given a tiny red sewing machine,
It's all stitched in mind, part of another past time
Which now remains locked in a nostalgia dream

Noël celebrated his birthday the next day,
We had our visit every year, Christmas eve,
Excitement built at the roaring old fireplace:
A world fired with love – and a child's make believe

But the big old rambling house wasn't quiet:
Especially at this season of pantomime shows,
My aunt took in lodgers and many girls gathered,
Their high-pitched laughter rang out from down below

Glamorous, friendly, smart, giggly, all so bright,
Dancers and stage actors, a long way from home,
Fascinated, I watched them, peeped through the stairs
Spellbound by thoughts of their strange world, unknown

But I learnt about life one Christmas morning,
Pure perfection I'd perceived - all gaiety,
Hushed: an urgent phone call arrived from South Wales,
One girl's father had just dropped dead, tragedy

And I discovered then both sides are constant:
Within our joy is contained a kernel of tears
And as the seasons rush on with old memories
This reality, sadly acknowledged, reappears

Lucky

Weird shadow witches danced on the curtains
As I lay drifting in bed, a few summers old,
Ushered by dream's embrace of all that's certain
Till a repeated uncertain panic arose,
When so young who brings children that burden
Of nightmare needles that disturb our repose?

With fangs biting into soft slumbering land,
Screaming midnight bleak fear – me calling out,
Taken then by the fire, my mother held my hand
And sobbing, I shared what my fear was all about,
"Why must I marry?" I just couldn't understand,
"You don't", she laughed, "it's up to you, have no doubt"

I'd thought it compulsory, yet don't know why
And in those small hour seconds my dark demons flew,
I still saw the same cloaked dark witches dancing by
But smiled, reassured, she'd said: "Just do what suits you",
So resolved and strong, I watched them rise up and fly,
I was three, and so lucky when my mum gave me truth

The Old Village

Just an old-world village, long ago, there
Were small shops packed with so much excitement,
One a general store, I recall the Mayor
Queue jumping, calling loud her entitlement,
A well-known snob, pulling high rank, unfair
In that lost world which held most requirements

Joy was 'Jack's Tuck Shop' up high steps, small door,
Just by the crest of that sweeping wide hill,
His 'Lucky Bags' held a special allure,
Tempted by his sweet trays, our mouths we'd fill,
Near fields, mown short now, that once brightly bore
A myriad wild flowers, beauty that thrilled

Down the hill we would walk past sandstone walls
Of Victorian houses, great styles too,
Deaf Mr Peever's sweet shop where I'd call,
Cottam's newsagent's toys and crayons drew,
The big haberdasher, I was enthralled:
Curved corner windows, silks, wools, every hue

The butcher's: pigs and cows hung out on hooks,
Down the cinder path his brother kept hens,
Green grocer's, antiques, Post Office with books,
Now different it has changed much since then,
And become chic and cool as time overtook:
Michelin restaurant, latest food trends

Over years the odd new house has appeared
Gardens sold for flats, a number of blocks,
Smart homes from garages, now disappeared,
Bijou dwellings with huge prices that shock,
Progress perhaps, but memory's still clear
Of the lost place and haunts, nostalgia-locked

Heathen

First day at village school, it came as a shock
To be the outsider, not part of the flock:
Un-Christian implant, sent to status quo mock,
A small heathen, church school, me planted amidst,
Suspicious alien imp, strange, devil-kissed,
A christening was called, said they must insist.

Was I there quite deliberately mocking
The institution of their God, quite shocking,
Confused by just whose big boat I was rocking
I bore the label, deemed a disgrace, 'heathen',
Which seemed at age five far beyond my reason,
Innocent, guilty, committing some treason.

Assembled to walk to church, the whole school herd,
Make me holy with holy rules, how absurd!
The date was set, my woeful state by all heard,
Holy water made a cross, then hall - huge cake,
By no persuasion would a piece myself take,
A Christian? Think the devil had first claimed his stake!

A Long Summer

It was a very long summer at six years old,
That July and August the sun never shone gold,
I frowned, weeks felt too long, and neither month hurried,
A new sensation nagged at me, I was worried

I was to leave the kind infants' teacher behind,
Go to the older class, where I was sure I'd find
Another, who I was certain didn't like me
And I fretted anxious thoughts that dwelt endlessly

I know the prospect, inescapable, rattled,
Fearing what I was sure would be a hard battle,
Those months dragged on, to later prove I was a fool
Because when I arrived, he'd moved to a new school

So although my young certainty made me so glum
Obsessed by a misery I felt sure would come,
I learnt not to imagine each day that's ahead
But live now, and not an unknown future to dread

Large and Small

Amongst rambling mansions where I grew,
Places of wealth and refinement,
I though, so well knew,
There were small houses on unmade side lanes,
Tiny homes surely of confinement
Which many children contained,
Where other families lived too

Sandy paths pebbled with stones, rutted and raw
Winding along to primitive old houses, unseen,
But those I saw,
One terraced lane was still called 'Dolly Peg Row'
Where once they'd washed gentry's clothes clean,
Pinned to clothes lines wind would blow,
Times gone so long before

Concealed, shrouded by old trees, far from the rest
Near nature's fields where our summer hours ran free,
Was their curious nest:
Diminutive folk, their tiny tumbling cottage stood once,
The Boslyns lived there, five, and without electricity,
Snuggled safely ensconced
Behind that ancient door, love-blessed

French onion sellers biked through those misty days,

And big brushes on shoulders, cycling dark chimney sweeps,

On life's disappeared ways,

Me in the middle, I made friends from both places,

All the same, and some across years I've been lucky to keep,

From old days, remembered faces,

As a long memory strays…

Hypocrisy

"Tell the truth, and never lie"
Hypocrisy church school spoke,
Did they count bribery?
It's prize, just a poor joke

Certain: her promise voiced,
Numbers needed, "if you learn
I'll buy you a book, your choice",
Words I found could twist and turn

In her flat, Saturday afternoons,
Recorder practice: part of the deal,
Learning those many tunes,
As her promise held the appeal

That day we met, I believed
The new comic annual would be mine,
But at the book shop, deceived
Found I'd been spun a lying line

My choice met her disapproval,
She selected the book she bought
And with that judgement, hard refusal
Turned my trust into cynical thought

"Tell the truth, never lie", she'd said
But the smiling headmistress lied,
Homeless orphans who had God, instead,
I read her nasty old book and I cried

"The good Lord you must always follow,
Be honest children and part of His flock",
Words I discovered rang so hollow
As my trust was broken and mocked

The loudest clear truth lay in action,
So I strayed then my own way, learning
With a growing dissatisfaction
Disillusioned and by that pretence turning

Bow and Arrow

Over the garden wall, lying there neglected
Next door's childrens' toys and abandoned bikes,
Aged seven I gazed in envy, strewn all uncollected
And hatched plans as I zoomed down the wood on my trike

Like a magnet those things seemed to be calling to me;
Every year the family went for several long months abroad,
They were indulged and I knew new ones I'd soon see
As those outside fell apart, just briefly loved, never stored

I was good friends with rascal George, the young boy,
Together we often caused trouble, got into many scrapes,
The weeks grew, I had my green young eyes on one special toy
And like a red Indian I planned its release and escape

Skirting their garden rhododendron border, I kept low,
Aware the visiting cleaner might that day have called,
Lying sad and neglected that lovely bow and arrow,
I slowly advanced, stealthily, near as I could to the wall

My dad laughed, next thing I saw he'd built a target for me
And like a triumphant squaw with joy, I proudly took aim
Firing flying arrows for many hours quite contentedly,
No questions about expropriation or words of blame

The family were still on their European holiday,
Summer days, blue skies, carefree times, weather hot
As they travelled without knowledge and so far away,
Over time I became skilful, then quite a good shot

I do recall I was enjoying living my adventurous role:
Dusk, crouched in the long driveway and well out of sight
Alone with the devil - mischief my propelling goal,
The road curved on the hill at that point, very tight

Then I saw him sailing past in his new shiny Jaguar,
Smart and affluent, totally unaware of my game,
The bend was sharp, so he just slowed slightly his car
As I emerged furtively, drew my bow and took my aim

I scored a direct hit! The car swerved, immediately halted:
I caught sight of suited beetroot outrage, in a flash
Over the garden wall I immediately vaulted,
Ran round the back of the house as I made a quick dash

Said to my mum: "A man's coming now!! - I just shot his Jag.!"
And furtively and fast I disappeared under cover,
Full of fury he appeared, like a bull who'd seen a red flag
"Is that appalling wild child yours?" he asked my mother

"Child? Oh no, none live here, perhaps try another?"
Not at all pacified the driver continued to loudly shout,
And happily for the little Indian, my smiling loyal mother
Said again "Sorry, but I've no idea who you're talking about!"

A Special Trait

Is it a special trait that we all lose,
Mystery possessed only in childhood,
Where despite us having no shared language
With certain friends we can be understood,
Then forgotten as adults, thought no use?

Puzzling now, when I look back and recall
We achieved perfect communication,
White and dark our skins of different shades,
Two children from two different nations,
Is this skill fully lost as we grow tall?

Greatest link from age six and seven,
Ori from Israel, my amber close friend,
Essence of an easy laughing union,
Long golden days close together we'd spend
And she'd cry at every Hebrew lesson...

With few words I knew she was my best chum,
And she let me watch her television,
We shared adventures in open spaces
In accord with no hint of division,
She spat out and shared half her bubble gum...

I wonder for her do thoughts still remain,
Is she somewhere right now recalling me?
How close we were, but without many words,
Is communication just what we see?
In her native tongue are her words the same?

As we age does this talent truly leave,
I question do we really lose it all?
As cold winds blow us through heart storms of life
Am I alone as I feel and I call
And send silent words that reach, I believe...

Ingredients

Mum bought me many great books to absorb and read,
Dad gave me my own garden patch to plant and weed,
Plus presents of packets containing flower seeds,
Which was all any small, keen gardener could need

Then he made me a small wheelbarrow out of wood,
Said: "Here's your own fork and trowel, with care it should
Soon be full of flowers, on this bare patch of mud,
But you'll need patience!" A lesson learnt in childhood

Summer, absorbed, I collected different seashells
Treasure washed to shore by rising high tide on swells,
Fascinated by thoughts of strange lands they could tell
I glued them to boxes, edged my bright plot as well

I had a tin, an exotic bead collection,
Fascinated, I gazed lost in introspection,
Pottery and glass spheres of jewelled perfection
And I swapped for more after thoughtful inspection

Daisy chain delight, my nail green stems would divide,
Make rhododendron garlands, which grew high and wide,
Foxgloves mauve, plucked, fingertip-worn, glamour implied,
Till I jumped: one still had a bee buzzing inside!

And when my bright paradise had begun to bloom
I had an impulse, a passion, to make perfume,
Baffled but intrigued, I tried, and failed, frustrated,
Ingredients of life, great treasures instated

Elements of our being, engraved, a soul shrine,
Deep joys we may know well as our instincts incline:
A good book, sea shells, flower blooms in summertime
That link beyond here, whispering essence divine

Nature's Child

I chose deep, high trees holding mysteries,
Tumbling green jungle, overgrown places,
Companionship in lovely cat's faces
Bird chorus ringing soft on April's breeze
And souls gone, alive there, living traces

Dark tunnels through rhododendrons, mauve, ran,
Secret: discovered a sleeping rat… dead,
Wide escape to green worlds, chosen instead
Of a prison indoors, much preferred than
Confinement: down woodland ways instinct led

Flower fascination, joy, enchantment,
My tangled kingdom where magic beguiled,
Antique greenhouse, ghosts' presence, yet gone wild,
Narcissi perfume, gold-white blaze, spring lent -
Dreams there for one then, untamed, nature's child

George

With yellow hair like a haystack, windswept
Into forbidden places we once crept,
The youngest, wildest one of five, unkempt,
We explored and both invited trouble,
A perfect infamous twin, my double,
So beyond barriers you and me stepped

Your wealthy family sent you to those schools,
The poshest ones, where you broke all the rules,
Exasperated, teachers you'd called fools
And soon from all you were swiftly expelled,
Amazed, with some awe by me you were held,
My accomplice, George, both untamed and cool

Marauding we went where no one must pass,
Our carpet green said 'Don't Walk on The Grass',
A magnet invited: 'Do Not Trespass' -
Building site, nearby intrigue, - those new flats,
Hours we mooched, rummaging in this and that,
Then your weeks in bed, particles, fibreglass

Gothic building, where bantam hens had been,
A fire – wood, matches, we sneaked in unseen,
Kitchen garden, cabbage leaves picked, big and green,
Intent: our bright fire we happily stoked
Until loud cries were heard: "Fire!' Fire! There's smoke!"
And shouting grown-ups spoilt our happy scene

I think about you George, life later on:
Villain, tycoon, ace gambler? Hope you won,
Is your hair still like straw, but white, not blonde?
My young accomplice, mischief alliance:
We laughed, broke those rules meant for compliance,
Our adventures yesterday, so long gone...

The Loveliest Thing

Scintillating vermilion – rare alluring sheen
Catching hints of deepest rich crimson,
Most beautiful dress I had ever seen,
A silk-velvet soft, spell-binding dream
Made from a glamorous cast-off ball gown,
Elegant then, I felt at sure at six, again now,
Necks and cuffs edged with lace in palest cream,
Sheer rapture was instantly known
Even though I usually preferred jeans,
It was the loveliest thing I'd ever owned

Delighted, I was sure in my mind
It wasn't just to be worn at party time,
Completely entranced, and determined, so
I wanted to wear it then and always,
To shops and school, but was told a firm "No",
"It must be kept to wear for those special days
Really only worn then could it be suitable",
And with my high wishes so undermined,
Which seemed so unfair and unkind,
That hardest line I was forced to swallow
By grown-up's last words, irrefutable:

I craved so long to wear that unique dress
On its hanger mesmerising, taunting,
"No, yet again, it's must be kept just for best"
Were the same loathed repeated words haunting,
Ever-longing, I was left unimpressed,
So tirelessly I tried then, by exhorting,
I begged, cried and whinged I confess,
Denial remained, set in stone, daunting,
But I was left very much more upset:
Because only twice did I wear that glorious dress,

It hung in the wardrobe, neglected luxury there,
Bewitching, tempting my besotted eyes,
(I still have a small alluring red fabric square)
Which in that vivid silk-velvet fast decades dissolve,
And although maybe that refusal made me later wise
By what happened: another year had evolved
With a new celebration, a seasonal invite,
A time to wear my lovely, red dress, I heard,
But it was then found too small, not still my size,
Everywhere was a bit too snug, suddenly tight,
Worn just twice, sure cruelty I knew had incurred
Which has left me with an unchanging resolve

Adored yet deprived of that perfection,
So entranced, I knew, in sad reflection
Tainted by my longing and its harsh life in hiding,
Crime for such a divine enchanted creation
Leaves today a deep inner recollection,
Which has delivered a long overriding
Very strong and sure determination,
That I would never use that statement to assert
"It must be saved for best", hated old words,
And be worn on some imagined future occasion,
With that resolve made, and throughout life, abiding,
If I buy new clothes, I'm positive straight away, I'll wear
And forget all that nonsense called procrastination

Remembering...

Alone in that big hall
Fanlight frightening up there,
Just about three or four
Sitting alone on the stair,
Remember how it felt
Looking objectively -
Wondered why it was
So deep inside of me,
Asked myself this question,
Young, but I couldn't say
Just how did it happen
That I cried every day?
And why was I happy
All alone in the wood,
Then forgot about joy
A life misunderstood...
Bow down with the breeze
Stormy days are ahead,
Run from the storm,
Don't choose life dead,
Should have listened then
Known there was a choice,
Melancholy dreamer
Deaf to her inner voice

Hill and the Long Road

At the hill top we stood and gazed up at the plough,
Countless bright stars, crescent moon brilliant, thin and new,
"Turn these silver coins, and make a special wish now,"
Transfixed - three were inspired by that wide timeless view,
"Just look at the beautiful vast night sky", dad said,
That same steep slope we'd zoom down in snow on our sled

Small triangular strange park, set on the high bend,
Puzzled why a short road stretch crest was called 'Mill Hill',
Did sails turn in winds Wales would reliably send
Blowing across from the west that rush this way still,
In times before had millers lived there and ground corn?
Pram-wheeled on unmade roads loved from since newly born

Intriguing, merchants' mansions built for those long dead,
Behind sandstone walls, my curiosity piqued,
'God first created a Garden' those big gates said
Beyond the façade my imagination reached:
Word-lure in wrought iron, no lie, what enticement,
Young footsteps trod lightly that road with excitement

I went too, maybe interest or just a whim,
That cub scout pursuit, they called back then 'bob a job',
At those grand gates, an old man, we caught sight of him
His welcome rare where there was no shortage of snobs,
Listened to our earnest request for light duty,
Then led to his creation of divine beauty

He showed us blooms with joy, some he called 'Christmas rose',
Wise gardener, shared his deep love, smiled with huge pride,
Planted in young minds small shoots later years could know,
Impression germinating ever-green, inside,
It wasn't work for us, but a wonderful tour,
He'd set seeds with such warmth, to grow on furthermore

Winding down the professor's dark path, overgrown,
Respected, at the best school, home of Headmaster,
But before the door opened, our welcome we'd blown,
The Housekeeper's fury sent us packing faster,
Our black footprints dirtied her white step when we rang,
Four feet ran in haste as were hotly harangued!

Further down the road from the village was 'West Knowe'
Set near houses once wartime embassies, they said,
Where summer-gold sun always shone hot when we'd go
Through whispered mysteries, and rose arches which led
To the garden gathering – highlight every year
For the small church school's big day, forever held there

At the school's grand Garden Party, yearly event,
West Knowe grounds in July, which I found entrancing,
An occasion all were equal and seemed content,
In best clothes: music, talent shows, country dancing,
Sandwich and jelly satisfaction mixed with blue skies,
With my wild flower arrangement, I won first prize

I'd gone early to collect them, loved and well-known:
Eggs and bacon trefoil, scarlet pimpernel, bright,
Buttercup, speedwell, heartsease, miracles, self-sown,
Arranged all in a round bowl, much to my delight
From coloured fragrant meadows, vivid memory,
It's just short grass today where they let dogs run free

How I Longed

How I longed for long hair
Loved a long time ago, still do,
Hair then was often cut short,
Called a tidy neat head, by who?
So those haircuts I would dread,
I just loathed neat bobs and fringes
My temper was often fraught,
Displayed in constant whinges,
They said too long was such a risk,
Knew nits could then be caught,
Back to the hairdresser I was whisked...
I saw the salon with hatred
Where they cut off the hair,
Shorn and mutilated
How I disliked going there,
Place with weird hair driers,
That peculiar nasty smell,
Women in rollers with odd curls,
Each time dread rose higher,
Deep torment for this young girl,
Wanted to give dad the slip,
Escape quickly from that hell,
What irked me most as well,
He said to "give the lady a tip",

The supreme indignity -
After what they'd done to me!
I couldn't do it somehow,
And give that extra reward
For my horrible shorter hair,
I rebelled, was not cowed,
And my mind flatly refused,
I found it just too hard,
So I couldn't see it through,
But worse, cross and confused,
Dad said "now please go back in there,
Smile, say a nice 'thank you'".
And it was that way for years,
I suffered, regularly going
For that scissor purgatory,
But all the while knowing
When it was left up to me
You wouldn't catch me there,
For a perm, rinse, tint or wash,
The thought my wild spirit goaded,
I've always known I'd have long hair
Untamed, unfussed, growing free,
Just think - that accumulated dosh
By rights I should now be loaded!

Inequality

What is the best thing that ever happened to you?
And do you feel unsettled on Memory Lane?
Scripture-crowded with holy saints, mine, Bible names,
On old school days, celebrated, frequently too

At those times a long snake assembled in the hall
To walk down the wide road, off to church, the way there,
How many of the flock – were led, blind, unaware
As they passed mansions, fine iron gates, sandstone walls?

I well remember – predictably every year:
Purple-white, cardboard boxes, 'collect for the poor',
"Those natives have nothing - we have very much more,
With Christian missionaries their salvation is near"

Canons came, regular as catechism and creed
And my mind wandered dreaming in forests and clouds,
Hymns and carols – "village children – sing God's word loud!"
But I witnessed unkindness in more than one deed

"Collect for our Jumble sale, let's get the roof fixed",
Both rich church begging and the box my dad hated,
In tears, a poor kid, one of five, castigated,
He'd kept a pram, poverty coldly shamed in our midst

What is the best thing that ever happened to you?
My church primary school could be a cruel place,
Though in that snake once, being counted, honoured, graced
A toad hopped from under a gate and pissed on my shoe!

Sweet Treats

Pastel cornucopia – rare seaside treat, yum yum,
Cachous, fragrant pleasure, on the top deck with my nan,
Trinket in hand, a small souvenir gift for my mum
And a horoscope: is that where my passion began?

Parma violets, see-through red lips, with perfumed tastes,
Thin banana toffee bars, surely strangers to fruit,
And Bounty, coconut dream, milk chocolate encased,
Love Hearts! And that curious dry stick, we called 'cherout'

Up the stone steps, to Jack's tiny emporium:
Glass jars packed with sweets, rows arranged along his bright shelves,
And in the big tray, Fruit Salad, Black Jacks and wine gums,
With pocket money we stuffed our small six-year-old selves

Blazing heat, a Jubbly triangle, nothing nicer,
Hot race to the Tuck shop for that orange frozen ice,
Or if flush even better, a Pendleton's Twicer,
Seven years old, summer, pink and orange, ice-cream spliced

Nanna would come twice a week, with a taste of heaven,
And eight years old, I'd run to meet her at the bus stop,
In her bag delicious sharp pointed sherbet lemons,
If not those, then powerful red and yellow pear drops!

My chain-smoking uncle called, it was not quite a cert.
That he'd bring me an answer to my coconut wish:
Brown, yellow and pink square coated scrummy Jap desserts
Or sheer bliss in all sorts of strange colours, licorice

Golden huge square chunks, so large, pineapple delight
And tins of toffee at Christmas, always too soon gone,
Those local mints, Everton, shiny, striped, black and white
Purple aniseed balls! Small yet that went on and on...

Told bubble gum was banned, it was deemed rather uncouth
And so that pink illicit sensation I then craved,
Chewing, Ori would take half of hers out of her mouth
And share, so I knew she was my true friend for always

Those hot summer holiday visits when mum took us
To Nanna's, I dashed to Stringer's, nearby small sweet shop,
In search of a sherbet hit, little bag with a big buzz:
Explosive pure joy - finger to mouth: fizz, bang! Pop! Pop!

Striped paper, Refreshers, Swizzles, swiftly dissolving,
Dolly Mixtures and Fruit Pastilles, did I ever stop
Sampling in paradise - endless goodies revolving
In young fascination with the enticing sweet shop?

And at nine I was drawn by hidden treasure un-glimpsed
Tempting me, inside a little Lucky Bag, unseen,
Though by ten, so grown-up, I then preferred salted crisps,
Pleasures savoury and sweet, childhood's great tasty dreams...

High and Low

The grand high church and much grander clergy
Preached ideals: "He loves you all equally",
But in truth beyond mere cant and pretence
Brutal acts were not masked by liturgy,
Young, but often I felt deepest offence
Hypocrisy displayed, seen frequently
In cruel starkest cold hard evidence

"Through us Jesus is here for you, living",
Claimed the vicar in embellished cassock,
"God's good word should be spread all round the world,
Show your love in our 'Weekly Planned Giving',
Then we can save those godless boys and girls,
We'll pray: children, kneel down on your hassock",
Church scheme, the poor to a poorer state hurled

Prize day was worst, always seemed most unfair,
Children with rich parents, front of the queue,
No reward for brains or ones in most need,
Those at the bottom ignored, kept down there,
Church parrot-chanting catechism and creed,
In sanctimonious belief they'd pass through
Those gates, despite lives of blindness and greed

Claustrophobia

Left in my pram in that big dim hall, under covers,
I found out later revealed roots of my deep-set fear,
The huge skylight above where ghostly shadows appeared
I was pinned under blankets, but who tried to smother
Me lying there, helpless, twice, a baby, innocent,
Setting the seeds of what brought inner soul discontent

I didn't know about this horror for many years,
Though rooflights in old houses made me feel I would choke
And being trapped in small spaces panic would invoke,
Overcome by elusive unfathomable fears,
Most likely caused in love-hate by a damaged person,
Split with her own demons of nurture and aversion

Over the old roads, rough stony tracks all the long way,
Pram wheels tested, maybe a rite, not baby's regard,
To the ancestor's place, stone cross high in the graveyard
Which rambles in nature wild, bramble-reclaimed today,
But I was spirit-absorbed, to my mother's disgust,
Though was I put in the hands of one I shouldn't trust?

Across the broad flat lanes I spent contented times, thrilled
By birds, wide gold fields, where birds sang songs into my heart
And always outdoors I belonged, felt I was a part,
But at the dark cinema, I could never sit still,
Spoilt everyone's fun, trapped like an animal confined:
Claustrophobia, infant-planted, clawed at my mind...

Cat Lady

They appeared and joined her, as I watched, feline-intrigued,
A family gathering ready for a nice forest stroll –
Fourteen cats of all shades & sizes, who lived then at The Knoll,
As onwards daily to woodland green paths the little group weaved

To smaller me she seemed like the Pied Piper, minus the rats,
My aunt, her summon whistling, and beret, how could I forget:
With bright orange died hair - body suit clinging, made of fishnet
With holes – 'tut tut!' frowned the adults, though no complaints from the cats!

She carried one small chihuahua, 'Judy', aloft in her arms;
Kept black bantams; amazed us all when a horse materialised!
Like a huge strange vision, we couldn't believe our big eyes,
Animals in need could beguile her every time with their charms

When a young girl she'd had a baby, such scandal then, un-wed,
Who her parents adopted, and so mute, she watched her growing
Unable to say "I'm your mother", the girl never knowing,
Who (coincidentally), became one of fourteen instead

I usually had crayons and paper, what I most enjoyed,
As she sat outside, I asked could she draw a picture for me?
She soon sketched the prettiest young girl's face, astonishingly,
When I showed delight, she scribbled on it hard - until destroyed

Puzzled and upset, shocked dumb, I felt totally deflated,
Looking back far, I recall such skill, revealed in that small face,
Was it her lost daughter, and did animals fill that sad space?
I thought I'd done wrong, but know now, life's often complicated

In those forgotten times food for pets wasn't even produced,
So to Jenny's fish shop down the hill, she'd venture to buy scraps,
Boil them up for her tribe, odd days, butcher's tripe, a treat, perhaps,
Cats prowled high shelves: anticipation, fish aroma-seduced

A white stray appeared crying at her front door, seemed propitious,
So grubby and sad, cold day, met her pity, I recall well,
Shock - soon after, she'd broken her arm on stone steps where she fell:
White cat, bad luck... her belief has since left me superstitious

No neutering was done back then – which occasioned my delight,

Though to some today this might seem peculiar, shocking and strange:

I'd often see newborn kittens snuggled warm next to the range,

But discovered life could fast turn to death - and found out one night

Owls on branches, daytime-dozed in great high trees, where rabbits ran,

And I learnt of animals' revenge, brutal raw tit for tat:

Under a window I found a young rabbit, killed by a cat,

Next day: same spot, rabbit fur, grey kitten dead, wrath: mother's plan

Homeless animals, my aunt was the one who always cared most,

She was like St Francis answering the plight of pets in need,

What difference just one more, another little mouth to feed?

I think Dolly still walks down those paths now, her cat-whistling ghost...

Aversion

Sometimes the lost roots of our aversions
Lay deeply buried, but are some innate?
Travelling on a psyche excursion
Back to the grim horror seen on my plate:
Maybe it was a route to conversion,
By that long ago which I never ate

Was the village butcher the one to blame?
Oxtails which grew larger and larger each week,
My share uneaten, described 'a shame',
Repulsed by the look of it and the reek,
A weekly feast - but my dread, this became
When a far corner I'd rapidly seek

Mugs of Bovril, they close-caressed, steaming,
My dad and brother made fully replete
As I dashed away with stomach heaving...
Proof one man's poison is another's treat,
Flesh early, I was seen to be leaving,
Is this why I chose to avoid any meat?

Loving the appeal and shy smiles of sheep
Doesn't mean I'm being sentimental,
Admire pigs' intelligence, charms run deep,
Bold presence of cows, eyes wild and gentle
And such joy of life, when a new lamb first leaps,
Reasons to sing long in praise of the lentil!?

My Great Grandparents

The wide rushing roads and tiny side hidden lanes
In my city of birth fascinated my mind,
With often curious, quirky and ancient names,
Dad once took us to visit The School of the Blind,
Both small, we were to look with particular care
And meet with the people working, and help select
A wonderful piece of wicker art woven there,
A special basket for mum, they were all perfect;
Along one road a shop was called the 'Wizard's Den',
A joke shop, with shocking things, alas, now gone,
A strong magnet firing young rascal minds back then,
The window was cram-packed with fun tricks and stink bombs;
And emerging from the tunnel, out from the station
Always the same pungent aroma hit was part
Of the city, a strange, unusual, sensation
Which came from the near shop where they roasted lambs' hearts;

Once a month – and on two trains we'd take the long ride
Visiting our great grandparents, some miles away
Out to a mansion-lined suburb, and the seaside
With four flower-filled lovely large parks where we'd play,
Mum would buy her divine perfume, made by Picot,
Tiny square bottles, French, either 'Train Bleu' or 'Suede',

Then down the long road we'd travel and lastly go,
Into the familiar loved haunt, shop called Satterthwaite's,
Meringues, sugar dusted cream crisps, coconut japs,
Confectioner's cakes placed in a striped box, then tied,
Never forgetting grandpa's favourite, brandy snaps,
Goodies that guaranteed grandma's smile would beam wide;

Our tall great-grandpa took us infants, by the hand,
Near their house was a railway level crossing gate
And with patience in anticipation, we'd stand
To see the train whizzing by, a flash, never late;
A dusty donkey engine, John saw it, smitten,
The junk shop - left a deposit, next month to claim,
Cleaned till shining, filled with methylated spirit,
Then marvelled with pride as it blew shrilly, his aim;
Going home, night-time, streetlamps and houses alight
Filled me with dreadful fear, so I could hardly glance
Overcome from young by an awful disquiet
With confirmed knowledge of our insignificance

A pub was opposite, they'd window watch and joke
In amusement, at antics emerging from there,
Their warm house was perfumed with great-grandpa's pipe smoke,

And they'd been together well over sixty years,
Both had been young in vanished Victorian days
And had lived through wars, and all the years in between,
Loved television, and were modern in some ways,
And quite thrilled, as they gazed in delight at the screen,
Both were always very thoughtful and generous,
So old, but they seemed to thrive and stay well, smiling,
We loved them both dearly and do know they loved us
And imprinted their memory stays, beguiling

Victorian

Victorian, my primitive primary school was,
Held up with religion, unfairness nailed to the cross,
Just three classrooms - central hall built of sandstone, and small,
Loose, sharp gravel stones surfaced the unmade playground then,
And guaranteed if knees hit grit a most painful fall,
Skin septic, embedded, like the familiar 'Amen'

Christmas came with the same play, tired worn Nativity,
Word for word unchanged, surely so like last century,
The cast chosen, babe laying in the manger, bizarre,
Us then chanting on repeat like an incantation:
"How far is it to Bethlehem, will we see the star?"
Practised at home much to my dad's clear irritation

Traditional country dancing with long swords made of wood
Held yearly at a big school, each team there understood
The event was important, encouraged to win,
To dance their very best in the grand championship,
Ralph, Alan and I had a small bottle of filched gin
So we three danced laughing, wild, as we secretly sipped

The Old Market

I held the handle tight, like an umbilical cord:
Cream leather, mum's big shopping bag, firm and strong,
I grasped that vital link where purchased items were stored,
At the eclectic old market, bustling bright throng,
Looked up at mum, seemed like a giant, and tagged along

I remember the long queue at the cheese stall that day,
To tiny me I'd stood forever and ever, it seemed
When my hand must have dropped down and I wandered away,
Expect I floated on small feet in an infant's dream,
Grabbed hold again, but saw an old man, not mum, and screamed

It was scary and think then I kept close by her side,
Shocking split, wizened features inducing sudden fear,
We'd go weekly to market, number six, short bus ride,
Just a few miles, which to young me seemed far, though was near,
Antiques last, aged lady puzzled me with her full beard

TODAY
WELSH
FARM
CHEESE
WITH
Chives+Leeks

That familiar shopping trip became routine, well-known,
Mum rummaged through soft silk oddments – a new scarf in mind,
Added to provisions in her bag, we headed home,
But divided, instantly bereft, up I'd climbed
On the bus step, it left, me alone, mum running behind!

She wasn't a giant I found as my height increased,
Mum's had qualities to which I can only aspire,
I still have silk scarves that she made, their charms never ceased,
If love is a banquet hers was a beautiful feast,
But that old market burnt down, destroyed in a huge fire

Points of Pain

Always bustling, place in the village to shop
The general store where most people would go,
Stand in the queue, inevitably quite slow,
Ten-sixty-eight, dividend number, Co-op
Where that huge man stood back so hard on mum's toe,
She yelped: "half of life is spent waiting", so rude,
He grumbled, no sorry, just pain for mum to know,
His unpleasant, impatient rough interlude

In my mind, always an unsettling dredging,
Searing hot day -indelibly deep-printed,
Dad's smile for me kidnapped, instantly hinted
Something amiss, he'd been doing high hedging,
I just knew pain had swamped light, that day tinted,
He'd fallen from his ladder, broken his arm,
Fretting I went to him, uselessly sprinted
For help, fear covered me, and love, such alarm...

Lost, a youngster with no mum, sat on those stairs,
She'd vanished, I shouted, but was not in sight,
Abandoned, distraught, sobbed in my sorry plight,
Told she'd gone to shops, couldn't find me anywhere,
She'd been calling, but I'd wandered out from sight
Far away, too long and strayed deep in the woods,
My own actions had caused me that fearful fright,
Explained with love on her return, I understood

Destroyed, I cried – I'd broken my sun glasses,
My first pair, red plastic, a swift repair craved,
But was told it's no use, they couldn't be saved,
One of those small pains that heal when time passes,
Like when I swung on the old wood gate and waved
Dad off to work, a splinter pierced, smiled anyway
Knew he'd worry, so determined to be brave
Cried after, mum got it out – and I was ok

Disease came, a duration none could predict,
Measles, stuck in bed, he stood and laughed at me,
That harsh act crushed my young ego, cruelty,
Pain the chain-smoking doctor did then inflict;
All ill weeks with flu, but just one day for me,
Six, down that lane on my own to school, thick sleet,
Storm winds tore at me battling on breathlessly,
Independence inside could not know defeat...

Experiences stay deep, by which we know
Joyful smiles can be switched quickly to sighs
And we grow, and perhaps it's then realise
That hand in hand through our lives these things go,
Humans feel other's pain and can empathise,
Know rewards of love can bring us great sorrow,
Pain and loss can make waterfalls of our eyes,
Yet with hope, our hearts greet the next tomorrow

Young Spirit

Was I a child, a nymph or infant goddess,
Verdant dryad or ancient returning sage?
Heart embraced by that calling emerald world,
Drifting along paths to another lost age,
Glistening bud, a tiny flower unfurled

I can see my young self as a small devil
But turn the leaf over and then call me shy,
Adventure, tied in with solitary dreaming,
Rules black and white created, made to defy...
Tangled hedge barrier to the park where I'd spy

Underground network of ruts and raised ridges,
On three squeaking wheels and gathering full speed,
Forgotten old trike I'd found in the outhouse,
Reclaimed - me on my beloved rusty steed,
But gnarled roots I found could a mission impede...

Down at the far slope, calling deeper to that
Half-buried house window where I'd mischief-knock,
But hurtling there over handlebars I went
Full into huge bristling high nettles: a shock!
Then searching quickly to find leaves of the dock...

All the true answers appeared wild, just contained,
Or were dreamt high on my adored sturdy swing
Which took me up to where birds perched and roosted
With a peace and freedom those old trees could bring,
Sweeping arc my fledgling soft song I would sing

The big garage – deserted, Victorian,
Used in wartime by Italian refugees,
Cobblers, then padlocked, left a long time empty
Sat silently cobwebbed amongst dark green trees,
Till a young handsome man arrived with the keys

Stan possessed a fine scarlet, shining sports car,
Needed some work before he drove to the race,
I badgered him with questions, conversation,
Kindly he humoured me with forbearing grace,
My presence not suggested as out of place

As he worked hard with tyres, metal and spanners
I joined his long hours as he fixed, waxed and wiped,
With paint box in hand, my novel idea to
Boldly decorate the cast iron drainpipe:
I did – transient thick multi-coloured stripes

I wasn't always in the deep wood alone:
Ralph and Alan – pals, were my close gang of three,
With stolen cigs. off Alan or Ralph's father
We huddled down low there amongst shading trees -
Matches: I'd skulk kitchen-wards, unseen to free

And we smoked together – three forest wild sprites,
Laughter, chatter and smoke rose up from low leaves,
Innocent: or were we conscious, and guilty
Of trashing what the older others believed -
And how much young thought can memory retrieve?

My wood felt like a personal blessed kingdom,
In spring yellow gold, vivid daffodil glow:
Two kids had climbed in from the park picking flowers,
Ran, told dad, he said: "Don't just say to them, 'no',
Say pick a big bunch for your mother, then go"

Heartsease, purple white, rare joy to discover,
Magical world – days long-vanished, where I played
But alive brightly still in reminiscing
And where I think part of my young spirit stayed:
Child or dryad, goddess or sage, forest made...

Wychwood

Sitting on the long road down at the bottom of the hill

Nanna's house, 'Wychwood', lived in for some years with her mother,

And she said "It's hard when yours leaves, but you won't know until",

She called her 'Moth': said sadly "but one day you'll discover"

Neat, kind nanna, undeserved challenges through life prevailed,

Her aloof older sister lived next door, unalike, tall,

Another, years before taught piano, music and scales,

Now damp, out of tune, still in the back room, against the wall,

And the roof leaked in that house which held shadows and echoes,

With paintings and vintage toys from decades vanished before,

Red velvet-lined, on arms of chairs, strange stuffed armadillos,

And when I stayed my bed was so high, I fell to the floor,

Old perfume bottles, long-empty, holding strange scents, no names,

From far countries where the sea captain, her father, had sailed,

Each child taken on a long voyage, but when her turn came

He died suddenly, further sad disappointment prevailed...

Dante and Beatrice print, next to a carved elephant, hung

By our beautiful ancestor's portrait, tranquil calm face,

Every niche held possessions of a life brightly begun

Which instead brought her great sadness and much pain in its place,

Pink nail varnish, she painted spots on Toby the tortoise,

And Buddha and Jesus on the cross, and how she loved glue,

Sticking and mixing religious icons, whimsical choice,

Teetotal, though hand rolled cigarettes, she smoked and loved too,

Ribbons, threads and lace tangled in massed coloured confusion

To mum's neat orderly mind, disturbing and alarming,

Fortune-telling cups, and world postcards stacked in profusion,

Which in nooks and crannies I found entrancing and charming,

Super-fine crochet hooks created her intricate work,

Designed and made stylish clothes from mind, all on a shoestring,

But in that house defeat seemed darkly impending, to lurk

And never ever the joy she richly deserved, did it bring,

Its atmosphere redolent, perfumed with her special charm,

Like her mother's garden full of flowers, rose arches and ferns,

'Cheiro's Language of the Hand' she gave me at ten, which brought alarm;

Then mum found some furniture there was riddled with woodworm,

So hauled it outside, smashed it to pieces, and piled up high,

She took a match, then danced laughing with her axe round the fire,

Pretty nanna, with lipstick and lace, however she tried

No luck in that house down the hill ever seemed to transpire

High Heels

High heels, "too young to wear",
Deemed a potential hassle,
A seven-year-old dream -request,
Their judgement I replied unfair
So was bought low heels instead,
At the front a dangling tassel,
Elevated to my very best,
My deep pride, in cherry red
Giddy more of heart than head,
Devised to put to a test:
Lofty, felt quite inspired,
"Watch you don't trip", they warned,
Those heels took me up higher,
Height of heel placated,
Shoes a ruffled fringe adorned,
Seemed so sophisticated,
A grown-up's world I'd joined,
Said never get me slippers,
My pet hate, a battle fought;
Then with skirt tucked into knickers
Enthusiasm had me caught -
Adventure loud-shouted joy,
My delight triumphed hope,

Arms outstretched at my sides

On that wall with pointed top,

I'd creep, braver than any boy,

Balancing act, pretend tightrope,

I felt the world opening wide,

In smart shiny grown-up shoes,

Wavering, but I didn't stop,

Favourite kick I'd often choose,

Tomboy well above the ground,

Looking from high, down at the drop,

I felt above the whole world

And in those red shoes I found

Dreams came true for this young girl

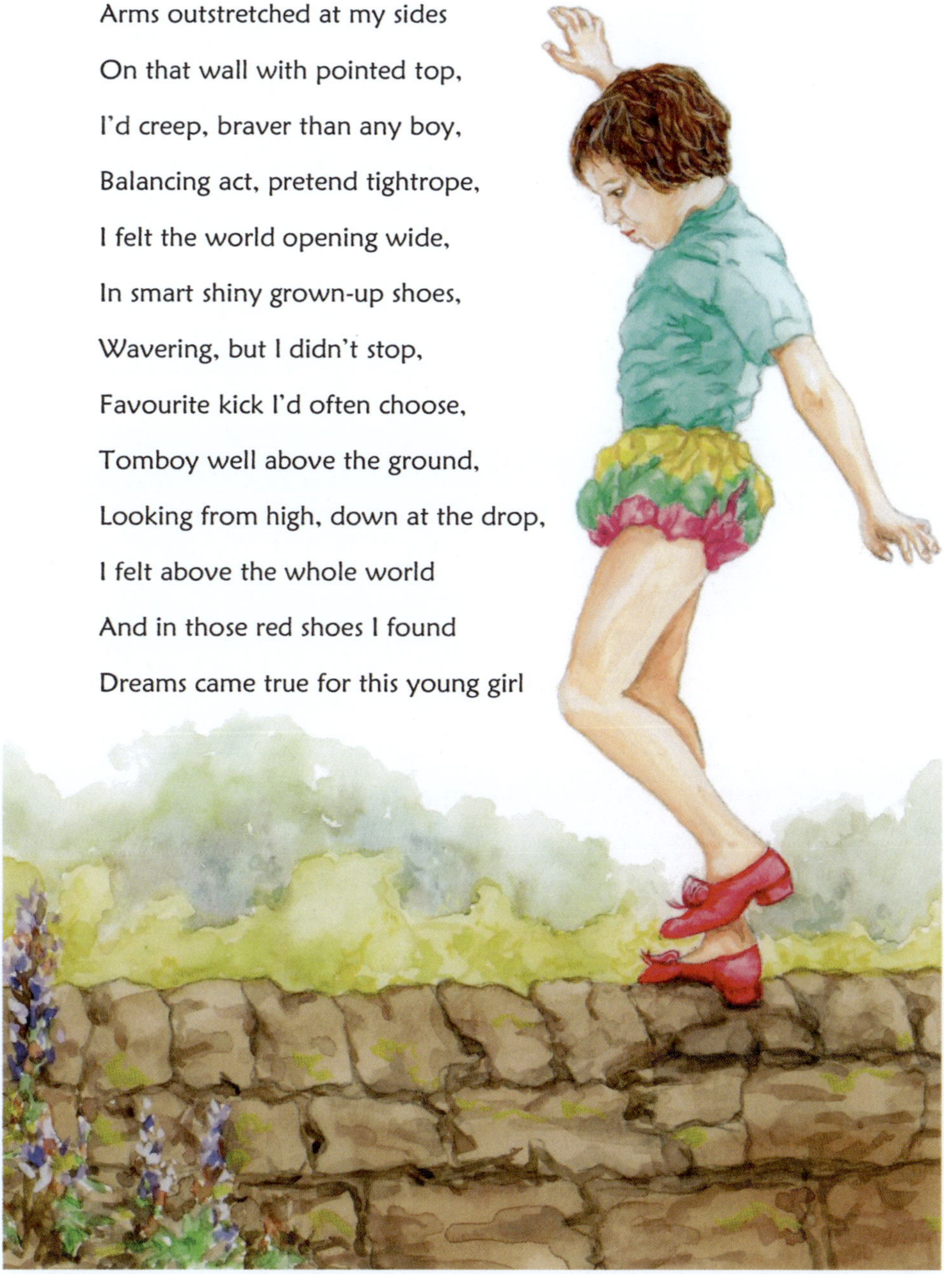

Creep

It's just a name on a bench in the town square,
Seems inappropriate, so who put it there?
Near benefactors and those held in esteem
Which suggests all seats are not quite what they seem -
Because that one commemorates a voyeur...

A peeping tom - I believe he was much more:
His favourite lair, the keyhole at the door,
Pale thin eyes transfixed in delight, reverie,
Spying at young girls bathing innocently,
Nude bathroom ladies he'd secretly adore

Along old corridors he'd silently creep
Unobserved, inappropriate date to keep,
The naval man, so smart in his uniform,
With his cinema room, grand but never warm,
Bland films shown, blue ones stashed, still waters ran deep...

Suspected by many, but never discussed
Yet found it affected so many of us,
He'd catch small me down in the woods with soft words,
Unrevealed actions, not divulged so not heard,
My Jewish friends left in his care, with full trust

Their affluent parents went on holiday
And left their youngsters in his hands whilst away,
Surely someone should have seen his true colours
Not waited years to hear damage and discover
A pervert-voyeur lived his dream free those days

The Joker

Discordant – school orchestra began, out of tune,

Glaring ice, the headmistress in anger stopped play,

Admonished cymbal and triangle, came in late,

Called the drummer boy hopeless, he'd quite lost his way,

Assembled and deflated in that lofty room,

Her disapproval swept through in a hushed ripple,

Silence; then William winked, giggling, my naughty mate,

Watched as her baton raised high: "And again!" she boomed,

He loudly shouted: "Miss! We can see your nipples!"

Shock! Suddenly halted – like stone we all remained:

No culprit admitted, we'd been well-entertained!

Two Friends

An old village school, very small
Same too with the size of my class,
Two friends were special I recall,
Exams they easily could pass,
And both shone incredibly bright,
Popular too, kind and polite,
But their lives weren't destined to last

Sheila bookish, dark hair, shy heart,
Ralph: more like me, impish and wild,
Destined, both studied, and were smart,
Ralph, big brown eyes, an only child,
Cute, - clever, fun, played football well,
His fate none could see or foretell
Blighted, that great future defiled

Ralph was a part of my little gang
We secretly smoked in the park,
Sheila obeyed when the bell rang,
Ralph and I shared laughs and would lark,
She had brothers - a large grey home,
Was seen often, reading, alone,
But for both life turned beyond dark

Hard to imagine future plight,
Saw Ralph later, just now and then,
Sheila once, gave her an invite,
Still shy, first time seen since aged ten,
Dear Ralph became sad as he'd grown,
Spoke sometimes to him on the phone,
Then never got a chance again

Life had appeared so sure, well-mapped,
Success unravelled, went under,
Sadness overwhelmed, and joy sapped,
Lives ended; I can just wonder -
If unable to tie life's strands
Surrendered by both their own hands -
Suicides – deep wells of dark thunder

The school is no longer still standing
Or playground of past childhood games,
Carefree young days, undemanding,
I think of them and their high aims -
Though plans didn't work as they should:
Shadows dance where we once played and stood
And fondly I remember their names

Show Me...

It is no different for women I feel:
'Show Me the Boy and I will show you the Man'...
Wisdom, truth set where children's patterns began
If recovered can our true natures reveal?

What use is religion and all that teaching
If proclivity is governed by instinct?
Young curious steps, inclination reaching
Down those paths, not what others wish us to think

I loved little Ralph, big brown warm eyes so deep,
His later life sadness will always invoke,
So I'll see him smile, a memory to keep
With his laughter in gorse bushes where we smoked...

Were other kids the same with their deep secrets
Hidden from grown-ups, known surely as shocking?
Exploration fun days, and I've no regrets -
Boys' glee at a glimpse of my Beatles stockings...

The wood ruler I broke, then hid, certain crime,
And bright paint water I'd drink down for a dare,
Fighting too, hair torn out, for girls, unrefined,
Raw tiny scandals now unburied from there...

With a ruler I'd fire soaked pellets of ink
When teacher's back turned, up to the vaulted roof,
Dark marks: 'Now who is to blame, what must I think?'
A mute class, supressed laughter, kept close the truth

And bored with saints, a ruler near, just a flick,
Reaction to dull dogma they tried to teach,
Black missiles my favourite diverting trick
Aimed above the line that the cleaner could reach

I swung like an ape over steps of old stone:
It was the way to ancient toilets outside,
Till I missed the girder above, pain, unknown,
My back, and limping I proceeded to hide

It's no different for women I'm quite sure,
We enter our private realms at a young age,
Memory reinforces proof furthermore
By the adult mask we choose for life's stage

Teachers

On the first day of school, a major event
I pause as I gaze back there in reflection:
Certain age, to the infants' place we were sent
With expectation of teacher's perfection,
On what was that based, a child's strange, skewed ideal,
Looming tall, like a giant, she stood high that day,
Her bleeze-blown frock made her human, far too real,
Saw her petticoat peppered with holes and frayed,
Knowledge font became a shabby flawed failure,
Imperfect, and gave me cool cause to wonder,
But heard Miss Evans was off to Australia
Saving hard for her new hot life down under

Though in the next class we all loved easily,
Neat Mrs Davies, her soft accent from Wales
Who read stories aloud wreathed in fantasy,
Captured us and entranced, absorbed with folk tales.
She weaved lilting magic: encouraged, enabled,
Taught us to read, at her desk, triumph recalled,
Showed joy with stones I found for the 'Nature Table',
Gave pleasure when she pinned my art to the wall.
Pretty, she sat at my table at lunchtime,
A calming peace her presence somehow evoked,
So I'd search hard for an amusing new rhyme

And daily tried to find and tell a fresh joke,
Just loved to see her pixie pointed-chin smile,
My use of pepper, she laughed – "Now all hold your breath"
And that is something that's stayed all this long while
But not Mrs Davies, so young she met death

In her tiny brand-new turquoise car, she'd arrive,
Headmistress in her suit, pomp with greying bun,
She lived quite near me but repelled me inside
And often called sharp order on my naughty fun…
I was floored by her dreadful halitosis,
Her disapproving eye was hard set on me,
Displeased, deemed me one of the most precocious,
Battle of restraint imposed on one who ran free,
I didn't know what had happened, purse, Snow White,
Rare, mum's from a child, I'd taken to show that day,
Somehow it had just vanished out of my sight,
Till years later, seen in her desk drawer the truth lay,
Any vestige of trust she represented
Went, though much later when she was very old
I helped, but sensed things hidden, a front presented
As simpering words lied once again, practiced, cold.
Only after her death the truth was revealed,
Her loyalty lay with a corrupt man, not me,

Affirmed my unknown suspicion, she'd long concealed,

How she used me, and lived beyond a century

Headline News

Glamorous and mysterious, her persona yet lives
On there, not lost to time in that big house: my friends' mother,
Blonde, neat, with her cute strange foreign accent, memory gives
Impressions of a mum, but so unlike any other

Unusual fashions, her own life, European ways,
Striking, but with a curious enigma, and distance,
A sculptor who painted and worked in the attic most days
Contented, but now recalled sadly in reminiscence

Lived next door then: an exotic, affluent life, it seemed,
As we children played, she was lost in her different world,
Protected, wealthy, but with her future dark fate undreamed
Which in complete shock some years later, we all read and learned

On their beautiful veranda, I had kind permission
To join them in watching the grand wedding of a royal,
In those far days very few folk had a television,
Spot of privilege with their kids, I was indulged and spoiled

We moved from that old road some time later, and so did they,
Travelling far down south – and a fate that no one could know,
To a picturesque cottage set on a wooded byway
At a crossroads, but then too soon she became a widow

Still young, sociable, she met a lover who was tainted,
An antiques forger: the judge said 'jail', called a heartless crook,
His face looked cold and cruel in the portrait she'd painted,
But she vouched his praise in court, released, got him off the hook

Romance failed, then appeared, met acting on a local stage,
A new man, and returning home, trees deep-shrouded in fog,
Both got out of the car, true love, just recently engaged
But were shot dead, the only survivor their mongrel dog

Tragedy discovered, the police said he'd gone to ground,
The spurned ex with the shotgun who'd lurked at that rural spot,
The one who couldn't face life without her, or being found
And by his own hand decided his end with one gunshot

Well-remembered by us, we read the horror headline news,
Unimaginable, such a short life for her remained,
Money, glamour, talent, charm all of no ultimate use
And they were both murdered there, strangely on Jealousy Lane...

Different Ways

Serious: a Grieg suite on your gramophone,
Or practising notes of choir music to sing,
Whilst I rambled outside, dreaming, and alone...
But those days we fought like demented wild things,
Wrestling and arguing, creating loud scenes,
Engraved glass table top went crash! Smithereens!

The parade of my pristine dolls, cast adrift,
Unloved, definitely not wanted by me
Must have envied your teddy, smugly he'd sit
Eyeing my rejects of plastic misery,
In wild places I'd wander with cats and stray,
Just two young children with their different ways...

We both had certain things about which we cared:
Various interests, hobbies, unalike,
New crayons – mine used, yours stayed new, never shared,
So upset I'd go off, on my rattling trike;
My gift box pen, never tried, you grabbed, it irked,
In bits, not put back, just to see how it worked...

FAIRY STORIES
Illustrated
Childrens
DICTIONARY

You formal with tie, me old jumper and jeans,
Perhaps predictive of our later attire,
Picture book scare – I taunted, laughed at your screams
Till mum ripped out that page and threw on the fire!
We were both stubborn wanting our own sweet way
So I chose other friends for easier play

That slow day, getting ready to walk the lanes,
Waiting: wriggling, hard to just sit still, so dull,
'Cute Thing' - bald doll, you loved as much as your trains,
But my careless knee smashed her brittle pink skull,
My crime: walk cancelled fast, your tears fell faster,
But she's survived, her head patched with pink plasters!

The purgatory of games, lives with me still:
Tiddlywinks: insistence you must have yellow,
Yet it's strange to reflect it's taken until
We are older for us to mutually mellow,
Those old childhood battles and all those crossed words -
History: we're quite alike, mutual genes shared!

With pages open like an old story book
I will still smile as I candidly reveal
Between the pages, where you're welcome to look
As the key to your library you often conceal,
Yet you tried to teach me violin by phone
And in time we've tuned in – late harmony known

Serious, but now laughing, you have helped me
With careless spacing and umpteen corrections,
Our foibles dimmed by years, inevitably,
Such patience displayed in search of perfection,
At Uni. they called you 'The Perceptive Prune',
I perceive now we play a much brighter tune

Connections

Strangers in a foreign land, but not overlong,
Not far to find a helping hand, nearby prong
Of the Menorah, tree branches stretching, roots heart song,
With answers and advice when something is wrong,
Familiar language, so isolation rarely known, or prolonged,
Saturday evening excitement, those times at The Knoll

Maybe not all orthodox, but religion still called,
Friends made quickly who ran local market stalls,
Came bearing unsold goods and gifts brought for all,
And abuzz with treasure being sorted, shared in the hall,
Life connections in new countries as known fate befalls,
Small dose of schmalz, though reality, and love most of all

His name was Haim, Hebrew for life, handsome, smart and free,
Woken at night, to say at once he must urgently flee
By his parents, who stayed behind in the midst of tragedy,
Aged sixteen, some money, a kiss, no time for uncertainty,
But to make escape, find the links that would secure his safety
Claim a productive future of great success with personal liberty

His ancient heritage kept deep, enduring brightly inside
Haim kept alert, furtive as he travelled, forced to quickly hide,
His parents' great love in him had a ruthless dictator defied,
And with his ancestor's blessing he tracked through Europe wide,
Then reached for the kabbalistic pledge and was not denied,
International 'Promise little and do much', plus a will to survive

So to me it was an introduction to a world quite unknown,
Strange alphabet, sounds and words for the Anglophone,
But confirming when strangers reach out, they are never alone,
And any region or place chosen can then be made a home,
One market item came to me, such a bold, fluorescent tone
Which I loved, a shocking pink top, a treasure proudly owned

The Arno

Past chattering bright budgies, dozens in a cage
Outside, route down the sandy, unmade stony lane,
I'll follow behind those happy child's steps again
Travelling looking for me at a younger age,
Metamorphosis of what perhaps now remains

At lunch hour from school, we were allowed and quite free
If we chose – to explore the close park – on our own,
Times gone, but in memory, remembered, well known
Wild places, high rocks, tall trees, to climb tirelessly:
Wonder, am I going back there now all alone?

Imprinted: tattered tramps on benches, makeshift bed,
Homeless, wartime sad soldiers, daytime, soft snoozing,
I'd disturb them, why? curiosity-choosing
To flout peace, and invade their privacy instead,
Not understanding, fool me, just me amusing

Girls from the big school sat grouped in a closed huddle,
So grown-up – intriguing magnet to rebel scamp me,
Boldly challenged them often, impertinently,
"You! Oh, why do you always come and cause trouble?
Leave us! You're a bothersome pest, just let us be!"

Trouble wasn't a school lesson they'd ever teach
I found it, easy to learn, running wild and free,
The keen gang of kids trouped along, following me,
"Let's all have a great feast on ripe nuts off the beech,"
But back at school I was scolded, punished harshly

Forty feet above ground, railings, on that slim ledge
I'd climbed, but late lunchtime my fearless courage flew,
Adventure – I'd gone too far, fear of heights, quite new:
Alone, frozen, quaking on that awful thin edge,
Previous daring heights I then instantly outgrew

My wood where I gazed longing, across to next door:
Tree-filled Park and meadow where the brownie pack met,
Told I was still too young to enrol with them yet,
Long-anticipated excitement lay in store,
That day they called me 'woodland sprite', I won't forget

Gorse covert when younger where I'd smoked with boys,
Caught grasshoppers in gold grass, tales could later tell
Of those moments, laughing with young handsome Paul Bell -
New pleasures, teenage secrets, we shared and enjoyed,
Fantasies created, for now, maybe, as well!

The wooden hut has disappeared where those tramps I'd taunt,

Victorian fountain too, which our thirst allayed;

Rose beds by rhododendrons, quiet, set in shade

Along that top ridge, where visiting ghosts may haunt

Place a bench in my name where new dreams can be made

Other books by Pamela Blanchfield

'Port Sunlight Village: its history, buildings & houses'

ISBN: 978-1-3999-5347-4

'"Why?" She Wondered' (for young people)

ISBN: 978-1-3999-5170-8

'My Moon Sketch & Note Book' (for all age groups)

ISBN: 978-1-3999-5171-5

'Horace the Hedgehog' (for children of all ages)

ISBN: 978-1-3999-4440-3

'The Cats' Hotel' (15 cats' stories)

ISBN: 978-1-3999-3415-2

'The Argh! Eek! & Yuck! Book'

ISBN: 978-1-3999-7388-5

Poetry, for adults:

'Show Me The Mountain Bright Meadows Below'

ISBN: 978-1-3999-2781-9

'Naked Love Tokens'

ISBN: 978-1-3999-4277-5

'Hurricane Heart Lines'

ISBN: 978-1-3999-6177-6

'Turning Leaves & Blue Fruit'

ISBN: ISBN: 978-1-3999-6760-0

About the author and illustrator

Pamela Blanchfield

My earliest memories involve drawing,
being outside and cats, and I was lucky
to grow up in a Victorian house
with a large garden and my own wood.

I was keenly interested in writing and reading poetry when younger, and this is something
I have again returned to more recently.

This book is my fifth poetry collection.

Printed in Poland
by Amazon Fulfillment
Poland Sp. z o.o., Wrocław

33930743R00060